"Draw your mom as a Superhero"

Copyright © 2021 by Porscha Chambers

All rights reserved. No part of this publication may be reproduced, distributed, or transmitted in any form or by any means, including photocopying, recording, or other electronic or mechanical methods, without the prior written permission of the publisher, except in the case of brief quotations embodied in critical reviews and certain other noncommercial uses permitted by copyright law. For permission requests, write to the author, addressed "Attention: Permissions" at info@mommyandmeswag.com.

Mommy And Me Swag
P.O. Box 33154
Granada Hills, CA 91394
www.MommyAndMeSwag.com

Ordering Information:
For details, contact info@mommyandmeswag.com

Print ISBN: 978-1-7363138-3-1

Printed in the United States of America.

First Edition

www.ingramcontent.com/pod-product-compliance
Lightning Source LLC
Chambersburg PA
CBHW081423080526
44589CB00016B/2651